OVERCOMING MY AUDIBLE FROST

THE DOWN & DIRTY

RACHEL EDWARDS

IREADWARDS PRODUCTIONS LLC

Live from *The Scout Awards...Audible's* annual honors for audiobooks, podcasts, and streaming radio... inspired by Harper Lee's legendary narrator Scout Finch in *To Kill a Mockingbird...*

I'm Jana Bakersmith.

For tonight's red carpet, all-star-sounding event coverage, my c0-host, Skip Words, joins us from the studio.

Divorce Games Network is thrilled to broadcast this year's gala- where audiences and contenders *literally share* in one another's stories. *The Scout Awards* offer rare opportunities for all of us to match our favorite voices and stories with their entire production casts. The *human beings* behind the microphones...many out of stretchy pants and studios for the first time in *months.*

The most talked about story of 2023's *Scout Awards*- isn't even nominated...or written, yet; in fact, Skip, it has only become known over the past weeks.

Divorce Games Network first broke the story that the author narrating steamy books for *Audible*...and telling exactly how she did it...was accused of being so cold and unloving her second husband physically suffered in her presence and could only survive with a married, disabled, terminally-ill woman escaping domestic violence.

If you think THAT author was wrongly accused, just wait until you hear WHO inspired her...not just to write, either.

Skip, can you *imagine* being *blamed* for causing someone to divorce you *and then* discovering an incredible life on the other side? *Because* those lies were actually the very script that saved your life? We'll hear and tell all about it, just once.

But not until after a word from our sponsors...

— I READ WORDS PRODUCTIONS, 1977

Fight.
Flight.
Freeze.
For those who need to hear the stories
From someone who lives to tell.
Divorce isn't funny, neither is adultery.
This book isn't perfect, neither is down & dirty me.
Write.
Elevate.
Sparkle.

We are where we are
We cannot control
What we cannot control
But we can fill our hearts with love
And share it with others.

As soulmates.

CONTENTS

FOREWORD

THAT'S WHAT HE SAID

By silently reading my husband's legal justifications for asking me for a divorce, avoiding alimony, and other winning defense plays, I questioned everything about myself.

Maybe I was a horrible wife and should have better saved my salary as a middle school English teacher? Moved back home with my parents and kept teaching? Walked away with nothing and never filed adultery charges against him?

He perfectly executed *an Audible Frost...fault me, freeze me, figure it out.* Well, *almost.*

Were we playing a game?

He and his agent delivered a *fault me, freeze me, fuck me over...*because one cannot *figure or understand* an opponent who disputes every part of a sport they initiated.

Dude, how many people do you think you are supposed to have on a team? You said you wanted to play doubles tennis...but you are wearing a helmet, want to spray paint new lines, and no spectators or line judge.

You've actually played this game before...and forgot all the rules?

Oh, you are mad I am making you play? But your friends say just to say you want to play and send me to the court? Then hope I just stay there until I forfeit? But we have to at least show our training camp contributions to play...what? Oh, I was on scholarship at camp. Ok, it's my fault you didn't make the PGA tour. Yes, yes, I will make sure to pay for that cart fee, too. How much money did you think teachers make? Completely...that was selfish of me to spend money on a classroom, spend time planning and grading. I don't know why people keep asking you for money. Right, you are going on vacation.

Was this just the usual trash talk before a sporting event?

"Plaintiff has the earning capacity to support herself. She has a master's degree and teaching license."

"Plaintiff withheld intimacy and was constantly on electronics and spending all of her time and money on online games."

Felt oddly specific- yet vague- and right on par for the next seventeen months.

What in the Wide World of Divorce was even happening in my life?

But while I was living in an apartment, desperately applying for remote jobs, shamefully relying on my beloved parents, I accidentally learned to produce steamy romance books for *Audible*, and far too good a dream career to be possible....but it *was*.

I just needed to believe in myself, not the "me" called out for Double Dare.

No longer being able to hide my deepest feelings of failure, anxiety, shame, and guilt, resulted in overcoming a trauma cycle I never knew existed.

I have an irrational need to please everyone, be perfect, and also perfectly selfless. When I can't achieve those goals, anxiety and depression result. Then, I feel ashamed of feeling all those emotions.

What I spent a year and a half trying to disprove in legal

paperwork and my second husband's mind, allowed me to hear the stories I needed to tell. If I could write the truth in the ways I prefer to view difficult situations- sketches, romantic comedies, or fiction- *that* would be *fucking* awesome.

INTRODUCTION

DOWN & DIRTY ME

Hi, hello, how do you do?
  I'm here to say a few words to you.
  My name is Rachel and I'd like to say,
  I'm running for vice president, to-day.
  Responsible
  Accurate
  Capable- that's me!
  Honest
  Easygoing, and
  Loyal as can be.
  So vote for me when you have the time,
  'cause, a check by Rachel's name,
  is the perfect end to my rhyme.

Fifth grade Rachel Lyn Edwards, me, delivered that speech from the stage of Lightfoot Elementary School in Orange, Virginia…the original OC, 22960.

I had painfully botched my first election speech draft describing myself and my family helped me write that last minute version. After Sunday dinner at Grandma's and on the front porch steps, my aunt Lex and mother dragged me through my character traits.

I then performed the speech from the yard until I felt confidence in my verses. They even planned my "winning outfit" black bubble miniskirt, leopard shirt, flats, and silver spray-painted *Maxway* sunglasses...yes, I am white-as-white can be.

My election speech- complete with parts of the horrible first attempt self-deprecatingly admitted and then finished off with the catchier, more confident, family-boosted revisions won the election.

Since I still can rattle it off with ease, I bet I seemed really confident and looked successful up there...like I really believed in myself. But I wasn't in the classroom to receive my victory- I got picked up early because I anticipated losing and was incredibly anxious.

That same experience would generally repeat about every ten years for the next thirty. Even though a lot has changed since then, much more has stayed the same. I'll tell you some of my story to get us started.

My name is *still* Rachel and my family are *still* my greatest cheerleaders. My parents, Skip and Janet, were both teachers and wanted children very much. My earliest memories are of my parents reading to me and telling me stories "out of their mouths."

When my sister, Jane, was born family life continued to center around us. We always went to church on Sundays and spent time with extended family. Jane has Angelman's Syndrome and continues to live with my parents through present day.

I loved books, reading, writing, and performing...maybe I watched and loved television sitcoms a bit too much or playing make believe outside...but I remember always being able to entertain myself and not quite feeling comfortable with larger peer groups or in social situations.

But I always saw the best in others and desperately wanted to be part of their stories...sometimes, I got scenes terribly wrong...but man, I always nailed expositions and initial characterization... for forever. Apparently, that's just how I see people- their best versions and I always want to be cast.

I grew up...and had marvelous adventures at Emory & Henry College (Bachelor's of Art in English Literature) and Dad bought four years of amazing friendships and Kappa Phi Alpha sisterhood...he joked, but he wasn't wrong.

I also met and married my first husband- he and his family are great.

After some brief graduation angst with my teaching license, I spent about a year and a half working for Victoria's Secret Beauty in management- then started my English teaching career at Osbourn High School in Manassas, Virginia.

When I am a school teacher- and I come from a very long line of public school educators and administrators- that's my complete identity and self...my students, their learning, and their stories. I am the *literal* worst at personal life/school balance. When I shared my career choice with my mother, no wonder she almost cried.

But I always liked to have the right papers to back up my mouth and ideas- and added graduate degree in Educational Leadership from The University of Mary Washington. I would teach high school and middle school English (almost all grades, alternatives, pilot programs) throughout the next 16 years in Spotsylvania County.

Despite having a son and marriage to a great man, I messed up and earned my first divorce. My mistakes, my fault, and my shame debt has been paid. According to our son, we are *good divorced*.

I then re-committed myself to my profession and four years later to a second marriage. What can I say? I have a life-time of stories to share.

But most future writings aren't going to include *The Froxics*. Folks with personalities so toxic and cruel- they become like dry ice to me. Honestly, I am over toxic person-alities taking away from the stories of others...why reward poor choices with attention? So, you won't find many future stories about certain characters in my second marriage- one liners, maybe.

This time...this marriage...I vowed...I would not fail anyone. But...I neglected to recognize the sacrifices to keep those vows and the consequences of silence. Much like my *Audible* experience...I was probably the last to realize the type of marriage I was in.

About ten years more... you will find me, Rachel...right back on that stage of 35 years ago trying to describe and assert myself...this time, it's a lot *uglier*, the risks much greater, and rewards for accepting failure?

Priceless.

But on with our introductions and into the stories I wrote during my journey Overcoming My Audible Frost...and discov-ering a person I never knew. While the narrative points of view and names may alternate, the stories allowed a whole new way of thinking to emerge.

PROLOGUE

THAT'S WHAT THEY SAID

They say the darkest moments are always just before Dawn. *They* say Hell hath no fury like a woman scorned. *They* say sticks and stones may break bones, but words cannot harm. *They* say there are *Seven Deadly Sins* and to embrace *The Golden Rule*. *They* say good people act specific ways. *They* say to always tell the truth in legal paperwork and court. *They* say all's fair in love and war.

Hmmmm…I had met all of *those* "theys" in my life. I had introductions through family, church, books, college, et cetera, et cetera, and so forth.

Since I have loved storytelling from my earliest memories, each "they" seemed to become a character all their own.

So, words and stories, became part of my inner dialogue, entertainment, self-talk, critic, and audience. My brain absorbs, creates, and performs words and stories. Possibly, irrationally, so.

A rational soul may recognize the word "they" as a collective pronoun sharing opinions, beliefs, or practices; however, I try to process each one as a story. When stories play

1

through my mind, I join them as a character. Or, once I understand, that "book" might be one that doesn't engage me as a reader and is left unread. I *see* the stories.

But if I am unable to create some sort of authentic understanding or achievement, I feel an intense sense of failure.

If I cannot internally read, process, and interact with their story words, *Audible Frost* falls.

After ten years of marriage to a man who criticized me into submission, I was silently screaming, drowning beneath the frozen surface of his cement pond of watery, self-fulfilling, vague one-liners of "Failures, Gaping Hearts, and They Saids."

He needed to divorce me because I had failed to fulfill promises of sex three times a week for the downpayment on a car loan he co-signed with me.

He lamented there was a hole in his heart that I could not fill. Even if I tried, he was confident it would be like all my other failures to satisfy him over the years.

They said I would accuse him of having an affair. *They* said I was a cold and unloving roommate. *They* said we didn't need lawyers because we made the same amount of money. *They* said he deserved to be happy. *They* all wanted to know why I didn't pay for everything in our marriage and take him on vacations?

So, I took all the failures, gaping heart imagery, and unrecognizable *They Saids*, and slipped them alongside their older brethren hiding in my brain's snowcaps and behind frosted tongue.

Sheltered by my iceberg casing and diminished awareness, instinctively guided by voices of those who loved and saw me when I couldn't: I moved, shattered, thawed, and unpacked.

As the granules of sand and litigation dropped the next

sixteen months, so would each phrase icing my spoken, written, and reading voices.

Turns out, when I am encouraged to be my most authentic self-and share the stories from my life-it would be both professionally and personally satisfying for me.

Literally and figuratively, I overcame *Audible Frost.*

CHAPTER 1

❧

COLD & CHAOTIC FVU

In the criminal justice system, sexually based offenses are considered especially heinous. In New York City, the dedicated detectives who investigate these vicious felonies are members of an elite squad known as The Special Victims Unit. These are their stories.

— STEVEN ZIRNKILTON

*D*own *& Dirty Post Note*: The title and introduction of the short story you are about to read have been adjusted to include additional insight learned between first draft and current publication.

Steven Zirnkilton's familiar intro and "Someone," are revised to respect mental health professionals, law enforcement, and all those associated with "froxic" relationships-especially children.

In most civil or criminal domestic justice systems, there are two sides to every case- usually prosecution and defense. In New Frox City, the frustrated detectives who investigate

5

these vicious froxeries are members of an exclusive squad known as The Froxic (or Fifty-cent-ers) Victims Unit. These are their stories- allegedly.

After watching all 22 seasons of *Law and Order, SVU,* I always imagined the biggest threat to my body would be a rapist or serial killer. Even as I binge watched the seasons over the hot Virginia summer of 2021, I made sure to watch Olivia Benson's changing hair styles and deepening plot twists with lights on or thinking my husband's robust gun collection or asshole personality would keep would-be rapists away. In a house as the only female (husband, step-sons, and son), I didn't feel particularly vulnerable. Nevertheless…someone was coming…

The neighborhood we lived in was relatively quiet and faces familiar. The lots were larger and many hosted established trees and even creeks. There was one entrance and exit for the hidden collection of houses. The changes within the family were almost completely imperceptible. The oldest two boys were preparing for college in August, I was teaching summer school, and my husband was out of town for various reasons. In hindsight, his absence should have set off alarms. But it didn't.

The communication during his travels was sparse and I can't say that I really minded. When he was out of town, the entire house seemed to breathe…or maybe hold its breath. Over the years, the house had become almost more important than its occupants. The front door was an eyesore…a navy spray painted metal door sans metal kick board hardware and screws still tossed over in the right corner of the porch…this was the third year of the infamous front door update (or security measure to repel would-be thieves)…the first two years had the previously red door scraped down to dull gray metal and paint shavings littering the front porch/door frame. Within the walls of the house, there were three evident standoffs with the insurance company... holes/leaks in ceilings, fireplace, bathroom walls.

It wasn't until October 4th that I realized my sullen husband's thoughts and ambitions were secrets from me. That Monday night in the third school year of pandemic teaching I first learned my life wasn't as I thought. After texting words of support to him about a job...his trips of job interviews had produced a tormented creature...and that evening I had sent text words of encouragement to him at work.

Me:What about going back to a doctor? I know you feel miserable.

Him:I hate my job. I am tired of being dirty and smelly.

Me:I know, baby. You need a change. What are the options?

Him:Take the job down there.

Me:Which one?

Him:The Chevy dealer

Me:This is about work, right?

Me:Baby?

There was no response.

When the man rolled into the house two hours later, it took him an hour to nurse American Honey out of a tiny stemless wine glass from an isolated weekend trip with friends to microbreweries.

That was when he told me he wanted a divorce.

The next night he sat on the corner of the stupidly large sectional couch and told me..."I want a divorce. No, there's no point in counseling...you can't love me the way I need to be loved...there is a hole in my heart...you can't fill it...you could try, but I know you would fail...I've been miserable for five years and you won't change...you won't snuggle enough...you promised when I did the down payment on your BMW we would have sex three times a week...there is no romance (because sex for a downpayment sounds sexy as hell, right?)...no, there's no one else and they said you would say that...who? the guys at Hard Times. I have made up my mind and I have to be selfish, for me."

As I heard those lines...failure and weakness coursed through my veins...and I could feel my chest collapsing around my heart...my shaking hands dialed my mother, son, and college pal...to tell them I had failed another marriage and I had no idea what I was going to do. There was also a chill through my soul...the man who claimed his wedding ring got in his way at work and turned up the tv to hear over any day stories I ever tried to tell...had delivered what sounded like lines from murder porn...

The next three weeks in October...not unlike the three weeks in October 2002 with the Beltway Sniper...were committed to getting my body out of that house...alive.

I dropped about 30 pounds between September and the end of October. Pictures from that time of college football tailgates show my eyes dimming and veins appearing beneath my chin...by November, my eyes look clouded and dead.

Separating a household of almost ten years of family blending, brutalized my body and soul. Thirty-two hours was all I had to sort, pack, and move...by myself. I did all I could and reluctantly accepted the help of dear friends and family...painfully, I realized that was the first time I had allowed people into this house in years...and they could now see the shame of my life shoved into corners and ammunition literally strewn around the steps. But I couldn't stop to break...something was coming.

The following days allowed me to start setting up my new apartment and one or two dashes back to the house to grab a some of the things left behind...I had tried to organize piles in the basement of trash…giveaway items…and thoughts of moving more possessions after my husband had gone through areas of house I couldn't reach or my body couldn't do alone. Entire childhoods of three boys were in that structure. Nine years of Christmas attempts…and failures, maybe he was right? I could see a lot of attempts to do things right and a lot of failures.

The Thursday after my move…I made a trip by the house that morning…November 4th…after I knew he would be at work…I was in and out in about ten minutes (just grabbed some decorating pieces I had left) and headed to The Dollar Tree…that was my unofficial therapy during this time (my soul needed to dispute all accusations of failure by working intensely hard to set up my own apartment).

A text message then pinged through my phone…probably after seeing me enter and exit the house by *Ring* doorbell… from the man I had generally shared a bed for 10 years…he wouldn't change anything at the house until I told him I was finished moving.

I knew the house felt toxic and sick after that last trip… and I silently had decided I wasn't going back into it until he had put some effort into doing something towards the divorce he claimed he so wanted. Physically and mentally my body was breaking…and I knew it…

I guarded my text responses to the spouse and requested he sort some areas and let me know when to send movers again. He quickly stated he would get to it the next weekend. Remember, he wasn't changing anything until I said I was done?

I wasn't going back…I vowed.

That vow may have saved my life.

Have you ever felt the energy of evil? An unexplainable force silently pervading your spirit and physically screaming to stay away from a place? I didn't realize that energy was coming...and SHE was seeking to take my life.

Five days later...I received texts that a woman who resembled me was spotted leaving the house...my husband carrying her suitcase and affectionately putting her into his midlife crisis of a car.

Without a physical vehicle in the driveway, promises not to change anything in the house and open invitation to continue moving the house...I would have encountered the woman. Yeah, she must have wanted that.

Over the next few months, I realized she had been ever-circling...nabbing hotel trysts closer to my physical body... once I was out of the house...she boldly crashed in. She was seen wearing clothes I had left behind during that frantic weekend move for Goodwill.

Like waves of icy saltwater in a ceaseless ocean tide, I realized the woman wanted my life...chills flooded my body. I had been surveilled for months... and didn't even know.

Much like the cryptic music of my seasons of *Law and Order, SVU* and Olivia Benson's deep commitment to survive the evil of each episode, I knew I had survived...just barely. Female predators are insatiable and my man with too many guns/ hole in his heart/rehearsed script...had opened that scratched front door to insanity.

CHAPTER 2

❧

WRITING GETS ME THROUGH MY FEELINGS

*T*odd *Bottoms...that name just feels like the perfect character name for the husband.*

After writing the short story "Someone" and sharing with a few friends, the therapeutic value emerged. Changing character names and expressing emotions in story versions released negative self-talk. As an author, I could see myself more as a character and less as a victim- it felt incredibly empowering.

The Down & Dirty Tastes of Betrayal-

But that wasn't where I was in November '21. I was in my apartment, confused, and still unaware of what had happened. I had scheduled a therapist and knew I was barely holding myself together. I wanted to break down and find myself. I lacked words to define who I was- just no longer wife, mother to three, or teacher. I felt as cold as how I had been described- empty even. I didn't recognize my body, but I felt it, and the taste of my own tongue. My mouth was void, earthy, stale, and a metallic essence of bitterness and the notes of Marlboro Menthol cigarettes I chain smoked as my own rebellion, escape, and reward.

The Down & Dirty Dialogue-

"Well, we've seen her."

Ahhhh, apparently, the neighbors had been treated to a show they didn't know they had been subscribed. The neighbors had been waiting for children at the bus stop and watched a woman leave the house with Todd. The car then promptly got stuck behind the bus and in front of them all.

This poor, unsuspecting girl- I really imagined his strange behavior must have come from a mid-life crisis with a sweet "Cupcake" of a doting young employee from his travels to a North Carolina car dealership...connecting for hours spent waiting on repairs across a showroom lobby nursing stale coffee in styrofoam cups...

And, there, it was, confirmation of what everyone suspected- Todd was cheating. I recall thinking it was a good thing I didn't believe Todd's text about keeping a key on the porch for me to continue moving items from the house. What would I have walked into? This girl must not even have a car. How old was she? Did she even notice half a house in transition? I tucked the visual into my spinning brain, a cup of mango margaritas for the walk, and retreated back to my apartment nest.

I stumbled to my mattress on the apartment floor; beneath plush covers and twelve fur legs. My son checked in from college by text. I felt the tears coming and frustration rising. I was too proud to text Todd any reaction that night. I refused him emotions, the only control I felt in any part of my life.

I sent Paxton the only phrase that came to mind- "Never choose a woman who doesn't make you a better man." If I was going to walk this walk myself, I would be damned if no one learned anything.

CHAPTER 3

BYRD IN DIRTYLAND

*M*y entire life changed through my cell phone in November of 2021- rather, through the screen of my overpriced Apple *iphone*. Eyes are windows to the soul and Alice's Through the Looking- Glass portal- Sawyer Smith unlocked my core through our screens.

But that name initially meant nothing to me or my fettered core. Just an alliterative noun.

So, who *am* I? Who *was* I? Who am I *supposed* to become? That November weekend, your guess would have been about as accurate as mine. I had no fucking clue.

Let's get that out of the way right now- I am going to be raw- curse, write about sex, and have to explain why to my mother. If I tell this story right, I doubt you will mind- but fair warning, we are going to be close.

Nouns, pronouns, and names simply delight me.

Expositions and introductions are as delicious in books as first sips of Friday night cocktails.

2021- most of that year I was Byrd Bottoms- wife, mother, and middle school teacher. That was my identity. That was how I described myself to others and assuaged my massively overthinking brain. It's a fulfilling life- I told myself, be happy, tomorrow will be better. Future plans will come into view, personal and professional goals will emerge, relaxing weekends, and friends. I constantly compared myself to others and critiqued failed attempts at who I thought I should be by 44. I had become numb, anxious, and unable to see beyond just getting to the next day.

I was Todd Bottoms' wife. With a last name that distinctive (maybe infamous), everyone in our Virginia town always recognized to whom I must be connected.

No one seemed to feel shy about telling me their experiences with Todd or the Bottoms family- yes, he has a transmission shop, no, that wasn't really his son, yes, he can be an asshole, yes, I know he's been arrested, yes, I know he partied a lot and fucked a lot of women, yes, I know he grabs drinks sometimes and gambles with buddies, yes, that's his ex wife, yes, we are a blended family and he treats my son as his own.

Turns out there were also name facts people didn't tell me until later.

But what I knew for most of the thirteen years together, was this was a second marriage and I was a "C plus" wife. I seemed to disappoint him at every turn- I didn't clean enough, cook enough, snuggle enough, make enough money, pay enough attention to him, want to be there enough, plan enough, want to have sex enough, have enough energy, prioritize him enough, pay enough, or have a job that paid enough. In truth, I desperately tried to meet the expectations that seemed marriage-reasonable at the time- I did have a master's degree, our finances were separate, I was obsessed with my teaching job, and I didn't feel like a good homemaker.

I had thought this was the home and marriage I deserved.

I really felt grateful Todd provided and wanted our house to be a home for our sons blended from our first marriages. I genuinely felt blessed he maintained using the word "step" just told people our business and it didn't matter. We both had joint custody and all parents were involved. There had even been a shared beach trip for my son's high school graduation- just that past June. We seemed to have co-parenting down and at 16, 18, and 22, I proudly told my middle school students I had three sons.

I blamed myself for my first divorce and Todd had seemed determined to marry and take care of us. At least that's how it looked from the outside- and just like the toxic house, nothing was what it seemed by the end. For now, we are slipping to the bottom of a different rabbit hole. Nothing good could come from staying at the bottom of that dark hole...and writing helped me start to sort out exactly who I really am. But one should never spend too much time reading, revising, and editing brutal character assassinations of themselves by a person who wanted only to destroy their character.

Hey, I can't fault Todd for that too much...he had really gotten into bed with an extra special type of person this time. I can easily see why he wanted to blame me for his choices.

CHAPTER 4

∞

THE DOWN & DIRTY SCHOOLING

*H*ow could I have lived with someone for ten years and never known them? Did I instinctively know and close my own feelings off in defense?

That Saturday night I quietly again sobbed myself to sleep. My son was thrilled to be home with me all to himself- and I was so grateful to have him there- but I had no answers or control over what was happening, and it was starting to dawn on me Todd Bottoms didn't care if I was alive or dead.

My attorney, at the time, also didn't understand my lack of details and fear of Todd- why couldn't I just stay in the house and find all the evidence for adultery or his banking information?

Because every cell in my body was telling me to run...but without names or details- what could I even file? I hadn't ever told anyone my married life stresses. I didn't know his rules and expectations weren't normal. I couldn't even get through a standard call with an attorney- let alone get on a stand and testify. I cried until I was asleep.

Sunday morning, I rolled-literally- out of my mattress bed to the bathroom about 6:30. My cell phone- always on silent- was swiped on the way to the bathroom, mere steps that were about to change my life.

The screen was covered with message alerts- voice mail, missed calls, Facebook private messages.

And, just like that, I knew who the woman was and exactly what Todd Bottoms had been doing the last six months. Sawyer Smith had also reached his threshold of tolerance. All of the messages were from him.

My first response to Sawyer was- OMG, I now understand.

Really, I didn't, but it was a name and confirmation I wasn't crazy. I listened to enough of his voicemail to understand Sawyer Smith was married to the woman Todd Bottoms had been with for months.

I shakily texted the number on my phone and said I was willing to talk. I stumbled around the apartment feeling suddenly overwhelmed.

Sawyer Smith called immediately and the sickness washed over me again- this felt horribly embarrassing. Plus, Sawyer sounded like the nicest person in the world. He was apologizing to ME for what our spouses had done. I wanted to throw up. Sawyer offered to send me whatever evidence I needed to help my case. I don't even remember the rest of the call- other than for some reason suggesting being buddies to get through the experience.

Perhaps a fellow over thinker or feeling somehow responsible for me, Sawyer agreed and for another unknown reason or instinct, hit the phone button for FaceTime.

The first look of his eyes- black, deep, sharp, and boring straight to my deepest core were unlike anything I have ever seen or experienced. Completely vulnerable, authentic, and real- he saw ME and I swear, believe me or not, our souls exhaled with recognition.

CHAPTER 5

✺

AWKWARD, AWKWARD, AWKWARD

*T*he days following Sawyer's first contact were *certainly* awkward. His reaction to seeing Byrd on camera was one of absolute shock. "You are absolutely beautiful. That's the dumbest motherfucker in the world. He left *you* for *my* wife?"

She was hardly putting sentences together and certainly didn't have a response ready for this man. Her voice wasn't one she had trusted in years and October had been an exercise in silence. She had been told by an attorney not to show any reactions to what Todd was doing.

Until she was out of the house, with a signed separation agreement, she resolved not to fall apart in front of him or tip the hand of suspicion. For several weeks, she even sat through regular dinners on the couch with *Wheel of Fortune* and *Jeopardy*. Ironic, wasn't it?

As she started trying to figure out how she had caused herself to be ejected from the marriage, her nerves were close to the surface and questioned everything ever told about her character. She walled off every feeling and shrunk into herself- physically, her entire countenance was flat and grey.

Words, spoken or thought, were high-pitched, fast, and tinged with almost a static...like through a phonograph or transistor radio. Sentences, stories, or classroom lessons felt fragmented and allegedly sounded like broken or disconnected. Her confidence was deflated and brain was overloaded...Rosey the Robot nearing malfunction.

Sawyer Smith was completely opposite of Todd Bottoms in almost every observation and interaction. It was evident in every technology exchange through their screens.

Sawyer noted every detail and said it all aloud. Later, Byrd realized he had also held back words and feelings in his marriage. So, sometimes, conversations were remedial for both. They were actually laying a foundation and testing every weakness; however, first, they teetered around learning themselves.

How he found her features interesting felt bizarre. Todd complained about her expressions and would seldom issue compliments- he certainly never empowered her as intelligent or beautiful. Maybe she didn't remember accurately? But all the years she was with him are tainted by the words and actions committed after he wanted her gone, blamed, and not pursuing a divorce- or at least a fair settlement.

Sawyer had barrages of questions assessing if she was aware of her appearance. Clearly, this *must* be a set-up that made no sense compared with Margo's and Todd's flagrant actions of 1960's flower children-esque love affair of months. They were unaffected by any concerns of potential adultery suits.

Byrd viewed Sawyer as a growingly safe friend and was increasingly unguarded with conversations:

"Ummm...dude...I have a messy bun, no make-up, and have been moving a shit ton of crap by myself- guess it's working for me?" Something told her she was not who Sawyer anticipated meeting as the wife of Todd Bottoms. She easily could have said the same thing to him- not a man she imagined being left for Todd. The man whom she always remembers as the nicest person in the world, clearly had been distracted from his original mission. Sawyer, a confident executive, intended to drop a data "bomb" on his competition and be done.

Byrd was younger than all of them and Sawyer always had heard affairs were supposed to involve one "fucking up" and not *down*. Byrd assessed a little faster that Todd and Margo weren't exactly the most honest judges of integrity or self-awareness.

Affirmations and coaching boundaries were established- they were friends and he was going to coach her. Clearly, both were uninterested in being sloppy seconds or consolation prizes. That was fine with Byrd- she could say whatever Mr. Rogers-esque mantras he wanted.

He was cute, but incredibly self-deprecating and they both were convinced something must be horribly flawed about the other. After all, they both had been blamed and rejected for the other's partner. But they did seem to get along and have a lot in common- far more than just an abrupt introduction no one seemed to anticipate.

So, she said his personal mantra- "We are where we are. We cannot control what we cannot control. But I can fill my heart with love and share it with others."

Okay, so Byrd gritted her teeth through Sawyer making her repeat she was beautiful with hand over heart. On Face-Time. She hated it, but since her first therapy session wasn't until later in the week, why not?

Why was she so comfortable with this man?

His mindset and way of thinking aligned with her own- plus, she didn't really know of other people experiencing whatever THIS was. Initially, she dubbed it "a surprise divorce." Even after final divorces were typed, words fail to

OVERCOMING MY AUDIBLE FROST

describe the lengths to deliver Margo and Todd their 10/3 and 10/4 of 2021 divorce requests.

After a few conversations and exchanges of Sawyer coaching Byrd "to confidence," she landed several intuitive call outs that resonated with him. They had quickly shifted into mutual coaching, accountability, and validation.

Why was this friendship so deep and absolutely *dynamic*? Their very souls seemed to join, reconnect, and *live.*

Byrd and Sawyer continue to support one another emotionally and intellectually. They still do their homework together. Whether separated by a screen, miles, or nothing, the foundation laid during the most awkward conversations of life, connect them as soul best friends- and neither is dim or gray.

CHAPTER 6

⚜

WAIT, IS THIS SHOW ABOUT US?

*S*awyer Smith has lived an extraordinary life. He is brilliant, successful, and everyone calls him the nicest person they have ever met. He exceeds and overcomes every challenge life presents. So when his childhood sweetheart and wife's narcissism became too insulting, Sawyer gave into his instincts and filed for divorce. With a bruised ego and an instinct for justice, he called the woman married to his wife's lover...and found everything he had ever wanted for himself.

Nothing made sense anymore and Sawyer felt out of control for the first time in his entire life...

A month after first contacting Byrd Bottoms (he hated the last name more than any joke could quip), Sawyer Smith waited for her to arrive at the small Airbnb. What was supposed to have been a calculated explosion for his cheating wife and lover- a married loser from their hometown- had not gone according to plan. Byrd wasn't what he expected.

What the hell am I doing? Sawyer thought as he paced the deck of the basement apartment overlooking the North Carolina view. The December air was brisk, but the sunshine warm on the brim of his ever-present baseball cap. He was always in control of his body, his mind, his business, his soul...and Margo had fucked it all up. Not only had she taken on another affair, this time she claimed the man was the love of her life and publicly flaunted her behavior. Sawyer could no longer contain (or hide) Margo's actions from their children- or the world- and it was humiliating as hell. It also pissed him off; he knew he was competitive and had achieved every personal and professional goal he ever set- except in love.

Sawyer had been faithful to Margo since he was 14- whether he should have been or not.

Byrd Bottoms was not a variable he anticipated encountering. She was supposed to just be the catalyst to wrecking Margo's delusional affair/life- you know, tell the wife of the asshole fucking his wife and make sure she had enough evidence to destroy the pussy in a divorce? For the first fifteen minutes of the phone call with Byrd, the plan was perfectly executed with Sawyer's explanations filling the air and only partial sentences of annoyance from her. But then... she strangely asked to be his friend...that was weird, nice, and something he would do. Worse than just asking to be his friend, she actually followed through with texts and calls proving she was capable of matching his friendship standards. Still trying to stay in control of his mental narrative of Margo's infidelity, Sawyer popped Byrd on FaceTime- and when he took her mannerisms, words, and face into his photographic mind- he realized God had been playing chess, not checkers. Sawyer saw his soul in Byrd.

They weren't supposed to be physical. Sawyer had made Byrd promise to stay on a higher plane of personal integrity than their cheating counterparts. So while he waited on the deck that afternoon for her to arrive, he was downing expensive red wine like athletes pregame carbs. He had tried to anticipate her every possible need...that was a habit he had kept after 30 years in the restaurant business.

The concept had generally served him well- anticipate someone's needs or desires before the individual even registered an emotion beneath utter satisfaction. Even though Margo had attempted to bastardize and weaponize all his own strengths against him, his success in business and public opinion often highlighted her cruel nature. But like most men who are emotionally battered by the female partner, Sawyer kept his thoughts to himself and just worked harder at everything.

His analytical mind, competitive spirit, and need to shed his protective cloak from his masculinity were converging once he first saw Byrd.

Byrd Bottoms was visibly trying just as hard as Sawyer Smith to convey self-control and confidence. She had also endured a difficult marriage of deceit and knew this meeting was a test. As much as Sawyer was struggling with his loss of control and past, she was unthawing her identity and awareness. Byrd knew from their lengthy phone conversations and almost constant dual existence- if sexual chemistry was present- they would be in elite company as a power couple.

Byrd had never known anyone like Sawyer.

She also knew his boundaries and insecurities. After all, he had been with only Margo and she wasn't sure what the hell she was bringing physically.

The first hour was the two sitting awkwardly on the deck. Drinking wine and shyly taking one another in.

The second hour was spent refilling wine and small talk about the accommodations.

Then...Sawyer requested to lie in bed and hold her... nothing more. The sun was starting to dip below the deck and the one- room apartment was comfortably warm. Byrd knew there had been sexual fire in their conversations over the weeks, but both seemed reserved and hesitant to show any vulnerabilities. She was going to make him feel comfortable.

Then...the fully- clothed- adult- snuggle changed energy. Sawyer took over. Without a word, he pulled Byrd on top of him. In seemingly one move, he tucked her head into his neck and firmly started squeezing his hands down her back. Both hands kneaded and mapped...exploring and possessing. There was nothing timid or uncertain about his touch.

He pulled his hands from her backside and back up her spine...firmly and fitting her body to his. Byrd's senses were muted and heightened at the same time...too many clothes and firm hands to figure out what was happening...but this *was* feeling physical.

They weren't supposed to be doing physical, right?

Byrd felt her mind struggle to process...this was happening fast and what if her body wasn't ready? Sex had never satisfied her and she knew had to remain vulnerable to feel complete.

Byrd hadn't even realized her body had softened that quickly for him, almost into oneness without any definition...warm soups of flesh barely held apart by fabric or threads.

"Be real," He pressed further in disbelief at her body's response.

"I am...can't you tell?" and then she realized he couldn't. He didn't know her body, yet...but by the look in his eyes, he was about to...

Byrd had assumed he would be a skilled lover. He noticed every detail of everything she ever wore, said, or described. Never had anyone ever made her feel so comfortable in her skin and with herself. Staying vulnerable in his touch was something she knew she had to do, but why was Sawyer so unsure of himself?

Still trying to make sense of what was happening in her now-fogged-with-ecstasy-mind, she wanted to get to his body. Unlock his pleasure centers and manliness, the same way he was coaxing her soul from the dark wastelands of regret to a sensual, confident being.

Looking into his eyes for permission, she pushed him onto his back and started tugging his clothes for access to his body. She only knew he didn't want any attention or vulnerability for his own need. Why? She wasn't sure. Was it about control or denial?

This wasn't at all what she had expected from this alleged "unicorn," had he lied to her or studied *The Kama Sutra* instead of cookbooks? Had he written it…or was this her *soulmate?*

CHAPTER 7

THE LADY BYRD BAKER NARRATION SHOW

Good readers create movies in their minds. Byrd Baker Bottoms, narrator of "FVU," remembered from a literacy mentor. God, she loved how people throughout her entire life had placed "gifts in her brain" to overcome the challenges of this season.

Unwrapping those gifts wasn't always pretty, so how about more of a romantic-comedy-literature tone for Byrd Baker Bottoms' stories? That genre definitely better suits the Byrd Baker of today.

"If good readers create movies in their minds, I should have a BBO by now," she thought. "Byrd Box Office." While still feeling somewhat like screaming silently beneath ice, our snuggle-phobe, was drawn into a TikTok video for paid reading. Byrd had been reading aloud for 42 years- out of her head, from books, in classrooms, back in her head... recording for money didn't feel like that much of a stretch.

Byrd didn't realize how much she was about to "figure out" with those recordings and productions.

The entire first production she didn't even realize

ACX.com was/is *Audible* and she definitely didn't know what she was doing.

The quiet of her apartment nest and solitude with her anxiety and massively overly critical brain? All her years of feeling awkward and uncomfortable with herself were about to change. As she battled through shedding trauma memories with Sawyer, both were recognizing how much they loved storytelling, family, and one another.

The Secret Life of Byrd Baker...she was finding herself reading in a closet with her dog. Even though it felt like an ideal dream job, she kept losing her shit when anyone asked her about the divorce or money. Every step of the process she had to initiate, finance, and accept- Todd Bottoms resisted, denied, and blocked. No deadlines ever met, rules followed, or adulting evident. Basically, made her pay thrice for leaving and he was a cheese who simply would not be folded-in. "Just fold-in the cheese, By-rd."

Speaking of cheese (not actually speaking about cheese), did you know how many careers exist for those specializing in the cheese industry? Cheesemongers can identify and tell the story of a cheese...like doctors of foods.

If you hand someone a piece of cubed cheese, they can taste it and attempt to tell you what it is. But, most people are nowhere close to a professional, just connecting other flavor memories with a labeled taste of identical cube. Without official cheese cube identified, one can only address impact on taste buds and feelings.

Byrd was all too aware of herself and scars. She'd been to doctors and Todd's attorney wanted those records to prove she had been harmed by him. (Motion to Quash...)

From her bedroom studio recording closet, she also wasn't positive if she was any good at this "reading stuff"... Sawyer, Pax, and her mother had all tapped out after the first book's prologue. It was too emotional to hear her reading about a mother with cancer. So, they weren't quite sure what level of narration she had reached by the seventh romance narration or her own projects.

She was starting to realize the recording process and combinations of technology may not be a "secret sauce" …it was feeling deeper.

Certain numbers gained more and more significance for Lady Byrd Baker of The Boudoir Closet that year…three, seven, ten, and twenty- three.

CHAPTER 8

CLASS, PLEASE TAKE YOUR SEATS.

*T*he stories our names tell are powerful. Names create images and descriptive mind markers- both our own thoughts and others who hear or see them. We may identify ourselves and relationships composed or presented within combinations of letters.

Right now, my name is complicated and maybe yours is, too.

Social media, *Amazon*, and *Audible* use Byrd Baker. Legally, and in most authorship, that's who I am. When I need greater freedom of expression or vulnerability, different character names or allonyms appear; however, they are always meaningful.

We all know other names and titles are still there- just silent, or unprinted.

Or are they?

When I chose to publish my first romance book narrations without my married name, it was out of spite.

I was spiteful because of all the memories and stories attached to being Byrd Baker Bottoms. Mrs. Bottoms, Mrs.

Bottoms, Mrs. Bottoms….in a classroom, it ends up sounds like Miz-Ottoms. One word.

I would much rather have been Mrs. Dobalina. Then again, I pretty much was, Mrs. Dobalina, Mrs. Bob Dobalina. Missusdobalina.

After each *Audible* production, I am asked to verify the name I want published-

Byrd Baker_____ (the Bottoms was silent.) From the moments I realized I was neither seen nor heard with that name, I struggled to give the word any part of my identity.

It would remain that way for months.

Surnames and first names are frequently used to communicate information- either desired character traits, lineage, or professions. Identify, prophesy, quantify, or rectify?

But what if the subject isn't reflective of that name?

A precious baby born one Christmas and denied his biological father's last name to escape a hospital billing system? A random word scrawled on a birth certificate to suit a con artist and devalue mother and son, alike?

Chapter titles with numbers that merely indicate reading order?

Popular period names revealing setting? Gertrude, Dylan, Ralph, Lyn, Dawn, and Marie.

Authors, editors, and storytellers have opportunities to empower and control name connotations. Note the sharp decline of the name Karen in America in the 2020's.

CHAPTER 9

❧

THE BAFFLING BOTTOMS EPISODES

*S*ome of the loudest words are the ones we see in print...

The silence of Bottoms' last name became deafening in hot July-something or other. Byrd couldn't close the divorce narrative because Todd seemed to baffle everyone with his anger and inability to agree with any documentation. Her frustration and confusion, even processing her own story and feelings, caused her to feel manipulated and unable to communicate logically.

We all know within divorce there are always two sides; however, what about when one party refuses to even participate?

Byrd was again dissolving into silent chaos and writing obsessively.

She was silenced by:

Words texted to a son she had been told she had to leave with his father-

"I will always consider you family also cause you helped raise me and I can't forget that. Thanks and I love you, too" he replied.

She vowed to change the narrative for blended families, names, and titles- that very moment.

Typed into a college essay about relationships with father figures and golf from Paxton:

"The man I truly considered a father figure, my stepdad, and a decent golfer, I thoroughly enjoyed whenever I couldn't play with my dad being able to play with him.

Now, when I tell you I have known this man since the age of eight, I couldn't even have seen this coming. Last October the man I called my stepdad out of nowhere one day told my mom he wanted a divorce and my mother and my belongings needed to be out of the house in a month. My mom was told there was a hole in his heart that she couldn't fill. Feeling bad for him, my mom packed up everything we owned and moved out. I will never forget getting that call on October 4th, 2021, at 10 pm- my mom crying on the other end- I assumed it was a relative dying, but it was her telling me that she failed me. She never wanted to put me through another divorce because of the way my father and her ended things. It turned out that hole my mom couldn't fill was put there by a woman he was having an affair with the last year of the marriage. The man I had known my whole life had been betraying my mother and me for at least a year."

Nine months later, the two encountered one another, at an evening golf tournament. The originator of the silent Bottoms of her name, spoke words of, "You've heard stories…they won't let the divorce happen…you'll understand when you're older"…and other attempts to fill in the almost year-long gap of life happenings.

Hearing the conversation from her son, she realized the pronouns Bottoms used created complete chaos for his audience. Who is the "they" preventing the divorce? Which story versions are in question? There were investigator reports, filed testimonies, and pictures on his own social media.

The look in this son's eyes was almost identical to the one she saw in the eyes of another son/brother last October- confusion, doubt, and disillusionment.

She was compelled to attempt direct progress/communi- cation through typed words the next day. Again.

More text stories: She could see past, present, and future in the exchange with the Bottoms who wasn't silent. The wounded inner child, mid-life crisis, self explosion, and rejected offer to help him sell everything and start a brilliant second chapter of his life.

Surname Bottoms: Let him sit on his own and tell what- ever he believes.

Bitter, shameless, and changing memories to make her the villain. If he must be the victim, closure can be within that awareness.

Byrd never wanted to be his victim, though, it would have been more familiar terrain if he had admitted some wrong- doing or taken some accountability for actions. She tended to blame herself, anyway. Prosecuting this divorce had been brutal and her self-esteem was waffling.

Was her character in question in struggling to forgive Todd Bottoms?

Well, he didn't ask her to forgive him. So, trying to forgive someone who clearly didn't want it and continued to hurt her with new actions? That made her feel like an idiot. Her name has been legally changed and final divorce offer just awaiting signature. Even though she had to pay for it all, it might just be worth it in the end.

But she could accept those ten years as part of her own story. She was punishing herself anyway for mistakes in her past. She could accept Todd Bottoms was just part of that and he could have his own responsibility for his actions.

So, how about getting to acceptance? Finally, Byrd picked out a few times in the marriage she felt he was good. She had witnessed those times herself and could allow them to remain unaffected by later acts.

After all, Todd Bottoms never actually knew Byrd...she didn't even know herself to share with him then...isn't that the way of romantic comedies? The villains become forgettable caricatures and stereotypes? If Sawyer and Byrd were the only ones who knew how those two had treated them, was there anything healthy about having a day in court? Did it even matter? The truth was painfully obvious to Byrd.

Todd and Margo never meant to get divorced...ick, they would have just kept Sawyer and Byrd as their *toys*.

CHAPTER 10

❧

LET IT GO, ELSA BYRD BAKER...

*F*rosticles: *Beliefs and obstacles that freeze validation. To overcome frosticles- identify, comprehend, and eliminate.*

FOR THIS AUTHOR *and Byrd Baker, our biggest obstacle was accepting ourself and cancelling the froxic review shows in our brain. Since we happen to have minds that replay scenarios and life in storytelling form- the comments of people who don't understand or know us, can freeze us. Especially, if they want to shut down a network.*

Now that we know the significance of saying, reading, and writing our stories, those froxic shows don't get many plays.

These are the final ones and best of the worst...

Coins, yep The Fifty Cents Frosticle and the numbers of dollars and cents my second-husband assigned to me, without much prompting? Yeah, the divorce paperwork and conversations with well-meaning folks froze me.

Since I had appeared to be fine and perfectly happy during my

marriage, few people knew what life was like with "Todd Bottoms"...
and no one wants to think of a loved one in an abusive marriage. I
was the perfect candidate for Todd Bottoms...one who internally
blamed herself for any imperfections and all his criticisms manipulated her views of being a good wife, mother, and teacher.

Just like the ways I was so self-critical during the marriage,
reading the paperwork and answering questions- made me feel like
I was undeserving of a decent marital settlement, alimony, or had
contributed anything to the marriage.

I felt worthless in all ways.

Plus, I felt guilty for feeling hurt and blamed myself for even
marrying someone like him.

Did I even deserve to stand up for myself and son? I put us into
that situation and I knew my youngest stepson was also struggling.
We had raised them as brothers for ten years...and I was completely
cut out- now being badmouthed through all the legal paperwork of
dragging him to court.

Few understood I hadn't left my apartment nest in months and
was mad at myself for even letting this happen.

I also knew a dream life awaited the end of this divorce-
because I was madly in love with the man whose wife left HIM for
Todd Bottoms.

So, since I knew life was so much better without Todd and what
he had done to me- did I need to have my day in court? Hold Todd
and Margo accountable? Because I certainly had all the evidence in
the world and folks coming out of the woodwork to share other
stories of their affairs.

Ultimately, I realized the adultery process wasn't worth it and
was causing me more damage than money could heal. I settled with
a one-time cash offer...paid for the entire divorce...and will simply
value myself.

You want to know what I was worth to Todd?

$23,511.50...

So, I guess you could say, I lost to win. But I have always loved 50 Cents...

Verbalizing, expressing, and reading aloud the phrases held in my emotional "autobiography," released me from the toxic mental abyss that almost drew me under.

Within the early weeks of 2023, I realized I needed to regain my own narrative and close the final chapter of my second divorce. Financially, professionally, and mentally, the paperwork and legal proceedings necessary to end the marriage annihilated my sense of self. Reading correspondence between our attorneys always highlighted my soon-to-be-ex-husband's determination to blame and shame me into divorce submission. Unless I would complete entire marriage dissolution myself, pay for it all, and walk away with nothing, he was not going to divorce me.

After carrying his words from October 2021, ten years of physical marriage, separation and divorce processing... settlement promises and a penciled- in-hollow-threat for a June 2023 court date...I recognized the weight.

All words- read, printed, heard, expressed, thought, processed- yoking my life stories and this one man's, were defining my self-worth and confidence. Absurdly, my value and worth, felt inextricably tied to proving I wasn't the woman he vehemently insisted I was in court documents. As a woman who always cared, possibly too much, what other people thought of her, it felt impossible to explain this marriage and divorce to even my closest family and friends.

Beautiful moments of my life were slipping by...precious days with amazing people...missed by trying to prove myself to people who wouldn't and couldn't humanize me with accurate characterization.

No matter what, I was always going to be a villain in this man's stories, but I had choices in the role he plays in mine.

Realizing the load I was carrying trying to shoulder responsibility for all the word narratives, I shrugged.

When I understood the impact of staying seated, standing changed perspective.

Rather than getting lost trying to understand a settlement counter- offer, I will cherish the opportunity to tell its story.

The Down & Dirty Class of '23
Freshman year spans 1977-2020.
Self-schooled, higher self-uneducated, unrequited.
Overshadowing a sophomore year, unexpectedly
the year I virally came undone.

SOPHOMORE YEAR STRETCHED 2020-2021.
Personally, professionally, cloaked in fog of chaos.
Breathing solely for those who loved me.
Undone by insults, instinctually escaping, the welcomed run.

JUNIOR YEAR REVEALED 2021-2022.
Vulnerable, real, and starting to glow.
Laughing, loving, learning my potential.
Dreaming, feeling, sharing warmth through stories seen.

SENIOR YEAR NUMBER 2023.
Accepting love isn't a transaction, stories are priceless, and my value doesn't have a sign.
But, if I must, ink my infomercial, return me to living, all for the bargain basement price of $23, 511.50.

CHAPTER 11

❦

WELCOME BACK TO THE SHOW!

he Scout Awards Show. Audible's annual celebration honoring audiobooks, podcasts, and streaming radio- inspired by Harper Lee's legendary narrator, Scout Finch, in *To Kill A Mockingbird.*

Entertaining Narration Highlights with Rachel Edwards in Order of Audible Release:

Nothing Like Him, Jessica Roe:

I didn't know if I was imagining it due to the whole almost dying thing, but to me it felt like there was some epic vibage going on between the two of us. It almost seemed…it almost seemed like he was looking at me in the exact same way I was looking at him. Could it be?

Scars On My Heart, Lynn Rhys-

Here's the thing. It's not that I refuse to change, it's just that I refuse to change for you. This is me. This is who I am. Instead of focusing on me, telling me how beautiful I would look only if I would make changes, how about you change your shitty attitude? I'm not changing for fucking anybody.

Safe with Me, Lynn Rhys-

His jaw is strong and square, his cheekbones high. He has

tattoos up and down his left arm, and his shirt hugs every muscle on him- and boy, is he ripped. His hair's dark and cut short on the top and shaved on the sides. This man is sex on legs. He's tall, dark, and fucking handsome.

Neighbors, Lynn Rhys-

Our tongues dance, igniting the fire that has been blazing between us for so long. Right at this very moment, we connect our souls. Our hearts beat rapidly against each other, and our lips convey everything we don't say. This is the beginning of everything. The beginning of us.

Treasure Found, Tim Grossi-

That trip was headed for Fredericksburg. After unloading and during their overnight stay, Virgil had been regaled with stories of the gold mines in Spotsylvania, Fauquier, and Louisa Counties.

From the Ashes, Lynn Rhys-

I roll my eyes. "No, you asshole. Normal high school has normal fucking terrible food. Rubber, bland chicken nuggets and canned fruit. Oh, and square pizza every Friday." I can't even believe what I'm looking at. My eyes don't know where to look first. "This is seriously the school dining hall?"

"Yeah, it is. Welcome to Darkwood. Though I'm sure more surprises await," she says mysteriously.

From the Darkness, Lynn Rhys-

Is there such a thing as a food and sex coma? If so, I am definitely having one of those right now.Also, I may be burning up, but that is solely because I'm surrounded by my men. My Kings.

Each title is a winner in its own way for lessons learned narrating. However, *From the Darkness,* produced some particularly cathartic moments. For that reason, expect more recognition in *Overcoming My Audible Frost: The Down & Dirty.*

We'll be right back after a brief pause for chapter identification.

CHAPTER 12

FROM THE DARKNESS AND OUT OF MY FROST

*W*elcome back to our show. This segment will highlight the value of using spoken words to release negative energy. Finding characters in books with whom you identify is incredibly important. Thankfully, many audiences realized this year The War on Libraries is a make-up field trip for those who missed the school trip to The Capitol.

Continuing to our next *Scout Awards* category…

Other People's Print Faves (OPP)-

From the Darkness and Lynn Rhys:

"There's a battle brewing inside me. One side keeps telling me to fight and do anything, whatever the cost, to get the fuck out. The other side tells me to bide my time. To wait for an opportunity to escape. But all of me is freaked the fuck out."

"Hold on for dear life and fight."

"Out of the dark, I will rise and burn this motherfucker to the ground."

"I'm not your anything, asshole. And you broke me. He doesn't get it. He's taken my family, my life. He's taken and used my body. He doesn't get my voice. He doesn't get the satisfaction of hearing me scream or talk. He doesn't get to hear my cries. It's the only thing I have left that I have control over. And that is locked up tight. It's the only fight I have left."

"Instead of being able to write anything down on paper, I find myself suddenly writing in my journal in my mind.

Hey Nix,

So, this is a bit of a shitty situation. No, no, this is a fucked situation. Totally fucked. I mean you're talking to yourself in your own head. It's not ideal."

We would like to recognize the advocacy, support, and applications of healing techniques for survivors (and thrivers) of toxic relationships addressed through the work of Lynn Rhys.

Through her characters, storylines, and books many of us realized the value of trauma narratives, emotional health and wellness, and accessibility for therapeutic educational resources.

Don't get your panties in a bunch, book-banning-burning-bullies, baby we aren't talking about you…we always take care of our biggest sponsors and business drivers…we mean through true literacy, mental health professionals, and availability.

Special thanks from our entire Scout Awards Committee and Family.

We can't wait until the Lynn Rhys releases *From the Flames* later this year.

We'll be back for our final chapters before intermission. But, first, please remember our sponsors:

Divorce Games Network, The Absolute Intimacy, Telling Stories Out of My Mouth, Hit the Spot Kitchen, ireadwards productions, Exterior Illuminations AJE, Profitable Selling Business…and of course, Audible.

CHAPTER 13

⚜

PRESENTED IN PREVIOUSLY HELD CEREMONIES

*W*elcome back to *The Scout Awards...*

The following *Scout Awards* were presented in earlier ceremonies and are still important featured works-

In The Technical Literary Category:

Yes, Virginia, She's Still An English Teacher: Frostcabulary or Frostary Terms

Audible- (proper noun) online membership service, platform, and company for experiencing audiobooks, podcasts, and audio entertainment. Due to its popularity, the brand has become synonymous with product.

Audible Frost- phrase used in work of Rachel Edwards to describe her trauma reactions in literary terms and imagery. Of the four oft discussed trauma reactions to danger (fight, flight, freeze, or fawn), Edwards documents herself most as freezing.

Audible Froster- a person feeling unqualified to narrate audiobooks for *Audible, an imposter.*

Down & Dirty- used as a figure of speech, idiom/slang, Edwards uses this saying to reference all the secrets, methods, or facts that might get her in trouble, draw negative attention, or upset other people.

Frosticles- limiting beliefs that require identification, comprehension, and elimination to overcome emotional obstacle or freeze response.

Froxic- a person who repeatedly exhibits personality traits intended to manipulate others and draw desired trauma responses. So toxic...they are froxic.

Motherfroster- another literary device and phrase...just in case context clues fail...the author always loved watching even the most prim wedding guests dance to Lil Jon's song "Get Low"...proving the point that when sounds make us feel...most don't even pay attention to the lyrics. Picture 70 year old white school marms...singing, "the sweat drips down my balls..."

IN THE CATEGORY of Most Underestimated Works of Advocacy and Self-Expression:

Nominations include these cheeky titles from 2021-2023:

The Fifty Centers Klan: University of Bottom Dollar Bets

Quality Control Gods: Personification Helps The Technology Go Down

Finding Me With OPP: Inspirations Through Other People's Print

Divorce Games Network: Calling Out The Best of The Worst

The Scout Awards: From Classroom to Closet

That's Just My 50 Cents: Sharing, Decisions, and Me

WTF, Margo?: Entitled, Ruthless, Shameless, and Dangerous

FINALLY, The Honorable Mentionable Scout Awards-

Recent Non-Fiction Publications:

Absolute Intimacy's Your Kitchen Inventory and Intimacy Inventory Workbooks, Rachel Edwards, M.Ed. and Karmaria Negron, LCSW

Third of Eleven: Jane Baker Smith, Rachel Edwards

Narrating In My Birthday Suit: Makes Cents To Me, Rachel Edwards (This novella provides the exact methods to narrate your own *Audible...just in case you want to do the same.)*

This segment broadcast has been sponsored by: *Spotify's Telling Stories Out of My Mouth...ireadwards productions, llc.*

CHAPTER 14

DIVORCE GAMES NETWORK NARRATIVE FICTION

*L*ike highlight reels, sideline interviews, and recaps from sports broadcasts, these are some of the best plays from the 21-23 Divorce Games Season.

I'm your host, Byrd Baker.

Even though we are still eagerly anticipating the final signing of our MVB, insiders have told us, that could happen at any time. Divorce Games Network asked us to proceed with our segment due to contractual obligations. But that's a perfect segue for the most memorable plays we saw all season...

1. Keep 'Em Guessing- Despite verbally calling for a divorce, Todd Bottoms continues to keep us all wondering if he actually meant to play this season. His agent assures DGN Bottoms wants to play and has everything under control.

Now that we have mentioned Todd Bottoms, audiences all tuned in during this extended season to speculate and weigh-in on Todd and Margo's dual plays. Many of you, suspect she designed their playbook...and I am right there with you.

2. Agent Ambiguity- Todd and Margo really nailed this

play. Agents and players did not share the same information…this allowed extra time, excuses, deniability, and blame. You have to admire this tactic when well-executed.

Play execution was also brilliant in early and late season games.

3. Self-Righteous Indignation- Some incredibly memorable performances from early- undocumented illnesses, internal organ concerns, hiding in plain sight, sliding coordinates and late season- evidence paralysis and memory loss.

It was *Magic Bullet Theory* meets *Gone With The Wind* with a side of *Dateline*…

4. Interview/Sidelines- Whew, audiences, these were some of the most watched plays. One never knew what to expect during these plays, blinding rage, verbal attacks, tears, or DGN Spring Break Affairs Gone Wild… so brazen and baffling. But we all admired their passion and commitment to the game.

5. Cash vs Credit- We sure hope our sponsors don't get any ideas from this one…fire up the credit card charges to use as leverage in settlement since it is traceable. Keep all your cash hidden and record keeping sloppy. Especially effective for business owners- limit amount of employees and paper trails, finance your life through business, file nothing with government…opposing team can't take what they can't find…and will cost tons of money to find.

6. Stay broke- Constantly complain about your newly impoverished status and blame the other. But see number 5…because you are the victim and deserve everything.

7. Victim Declarations- People don't want to blame a victim, so always be the victim. Everyone was, is, and will be out to get you. If you start to feel bad about your tactics, remember what the other person made you do, is going to cost you, and they abandoned/left you. It is not your fault. They made you act this way. People tried to warn them.

8. Manipulate Pain Points-Make them feel sorry for you by pushing buttons on whatever they care about most. You want them to give in. If your opponents aren't up for the fight, why'd they even start it? Trick play...you started it, but blame 'em anyway.

9. Manipulative Child's Play- Tell any kids involved they aren't responsible for divorce. Then manipulate their feelings about the other party and play the victim. Make kids feel guilty for any evaluations, assessments, or processing of what they may have witnessed. Tell them only what you want them to believe. Use the kids and your place in their life to overcome the other party. Everyone who can breathe is either with you or consider them against you. Talking equals telling. Nothing was your fault, remember?

10. Drag Those Feet- be unavailable, out of town, unresponsive, vague, noncommittal with deadlines, sick, overworked, heading out of town, etc, etc, and so forth. If it isn't something you want to do or will cost you something, avoid it. Stay out of all courtrooms.

11. Baffle, Baffle, Slide The Shells- Finally, offer a random sum, sell everything, declare bankruptcy, pocket all cash and move. Blame it all on everyone else, repeat.

12. Loud Wailing/Coming In Hot- When all else fails, go with surprise accusations and sneak attacks during times no one would anticipate. Shock and awe, baby! The less likely someone wants to admit being married to you- the more you score!

Wow, those could be some ruthless plays, thank goodness our writers have been unable to confirm sources. I am not sure if anyone in this *Wide World of Divorce Sports* is ready to have fans or followers for these characters.

For Divorce Games Network,
Byrd Baker

CHAPTER 15

❧

THE MIDDLE AGE AFTER MIDDLE SCHOOL SPECIAL

*W*hat if you were suddenly bound by a promise scrawled in your middle school yearbook from the 1980s? One of those "first to sign your crack,"..." your/you're cute,"..."never change, don't forget to write, call me sometime 555-4179, ttyl, stay cool this summer, hope we have more classes together, never forget CoEd Naked Fire-fighting: Find 'Em Hot, Leave 'Em Wet, never break up with Michele E. or I'll break your face" yearbooks before they cost $79 dollars in modern day varieties.

Sissy Bottoms (something-or-the-other-now) was staring down at words she had almost forgotten writing in a *Battlefield Middle School* yearbook from 1987...and beside the floppy cursive writing typical of girls of the day...were two brown smudges marking her own and middle school best friend's blood pact.

LYLS, BFFs, BBF, WMG4L...sis by 50 or die trying, 'cuz your bro's hot!!!!!- SB/MLB hahaha

Love you like a sister. Best Friends Forever. Badass

Bitches. Warrior Mean Girls For Life...Sissy Bottoms and Margo Little Bottoms.

Sissy looked from the page to the friend who had brought the book to her father's milestone birthday weekend. *Margo.*

Holy Shitballs...and her brother was heading that way. No longer was he the high school senior mentioned in that yearbook. Nor were they the same girls who ruled that middle school and loved shocking everyone with their antics. Margo would always say whatever she wanted and never cared who she hurt, made fun of, or got in her way...the world was her playground...you were either with her or declared an enemy to be taken out.

"Shit, Margo...you serious? Girl, you both are married." Sissy halfway cautioned...she knew to that very day, Margo never missed any opportunities for girls vacations, drinking too much, showing off whatever she could get away with- no one questioned her or there was hell to pay.

Some say middle school mean girls never change, they just get meaner. Oh, yeah, that might have been them...and life was boring after a pandemic.

"Well, sounds *exciting* to me...and *who* can argue with something we pledged with a blood oath? *If our spouses cared what we did, where the fuck are they? Who misses a father's birthday of skydiving? I'll show you all how to live. Shit, and I'm even here after having surgery. If I won't let disability or work keep me away? They are the losers working instead of celebrating life.*"

"I think Todd said something about her having to teach summer school."

"So, she's a teacher? *That's even better...*I always loved pissing off teachers and Sawyer's always working and making me feel bad. *Like a principal...and we always loved getting away with shit, Sissy.*"

"Yeah, but what if you do get caught?" Sissy was warming to fun of it all...those were fun years in middle school and Margo was always over the top. Who wouldn't want to go back to middle school and have her brother with her middle school bestie? *Plus, skydiving with their whole family?*

"I'll take care of it all...if I can get with Todd Bottoms after all of those rumors we always heard? *I'll just tell him what to say to his cold bitch and scare the pension right the fuck out of goody-two-shoes Sawyer. This will be fun and hot. Even if we get caught, those fools would have to prove it anyway...and then I would just play crazy...who would ever divorce the most fun people like us? Who can prove my sickness didn't just get better for awhile, anyway...like an act of God or a miracle? Mean girls always win...or let those fuckers do all the work anyway. No one would ever believe we planned this for an old man's birthday party...y'all always threw the best parties!"*

Ignoring all the slight chills down her spine and looking back at her old yearbook Margo had packed for this trip, Sissy figured, "What the hell, we only live once and her BFF always seemed to land on her feet... those poor fools had to have known who they were marrying with Margo and Todd...you get what you get, right?"

Because she sure as fuck didn't want to see Margo throw a fit or turn on her. She also wasn't quite sure Margo had realized the name thing...

On behalf of all of us at Divorce Games Network, do you know where your middle school yearbooks are located?

EPILOGUE

JUST MY 50 CENTS

llusions, credits, copyrights, permissions have all been given, granted, or will be asked for forgiveness. Literally, my brain reframes difficult situations into humorous comparisons.

So, as we wrap up this franchise installment, let's go back to where we started-

Holiday roads...no, not all those vacations our spouses took together- skydiving, beach, and with Bottoms, Bells, and Badger families. Maybe they thought it was like the rotations of actors for Russ & Audrey?

But the holidays and roads that can't be charged on credit... because Chris Harris and I had never considered ourselves victims of anything until having to execute both of these divorces. So, despite Todd and Margo causing our introduction- roads now divide into our stories, not theirs.

We have covered enough of their characters- it's pretty brutal to realize you married the types of people who cause warning labels and heinous "victimless" crimes.

We have travelled roads...some of the biggest roads of life and responsibilities we never expected to share with another...without even needing words. Which is the gift that keeps on giving...and I am forever grateful.

But, since he was born on Christmas Day, given a name other than his father's by his father, and been crucified for money...I can see why I paid for a divorce that included coins of silver. I am so grateful for my family, friends, attorney, therapist, and soul family.

Yep, I rolled up to the banking shop to cash three checks that could not even be rounded up to the nearest dollar.

Our pasts are prologue
The epilogue our exposition
And our fruits are the
Nectar for a legacy loved.

Overcoming my audible frost and recognizing the "down and dirty" truths will always be part of this story. I found growth and healing by reframing negative experiences. By completing all stages of the divorce grieving stages, I found the closure Todd would never grant. Allowing the "ugly" writing and sarcasm to show through as I came to terms with these divorces? Yes, that was my own assignment.

I learned my lessons and passed my class. As for Todd Bottoms, he skipped every session and can kiss my…

The End.

www.ingramcontent.com/pod-product-compliance
Lightning Source LLC
Chambersburg PA
CBHW032053040426
42449CB00007B/1092